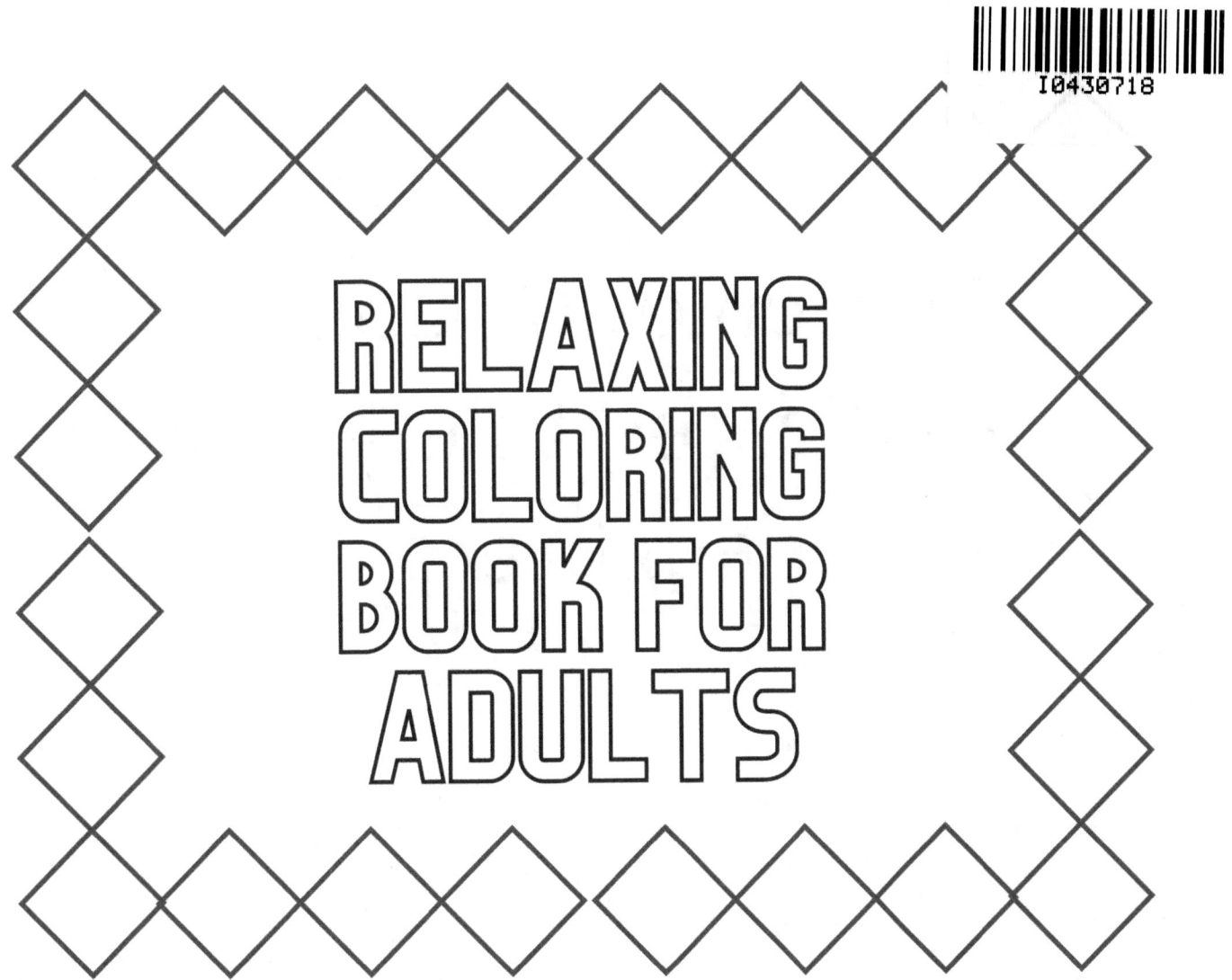

Original Drawings designed specifically to help you relax and enjoy coloring!

©2022 Stephanie Nicole Trentham

This coloring book is dedicated to my two daughters.

©2022 Stephanie Nicole Trentham

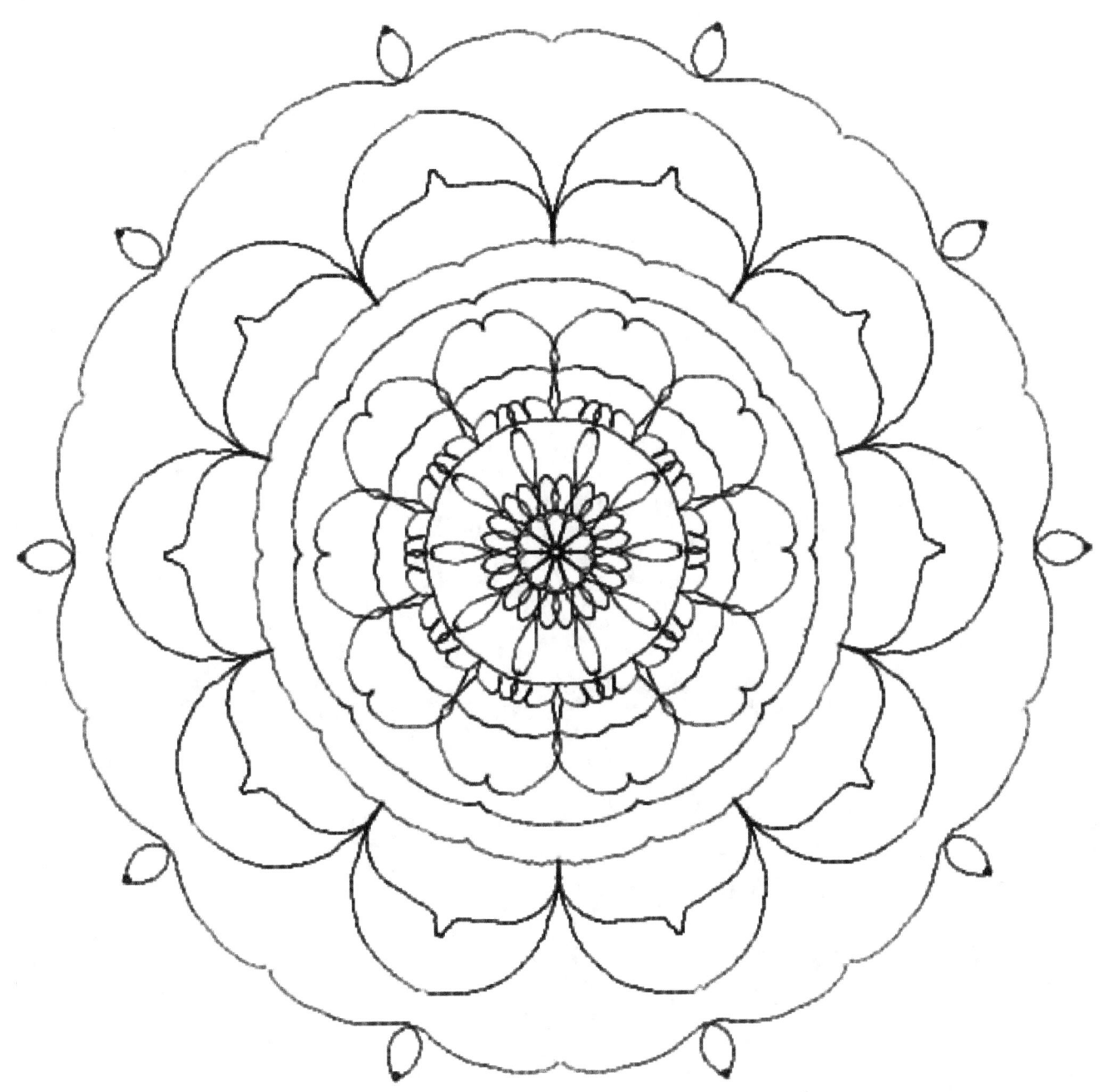

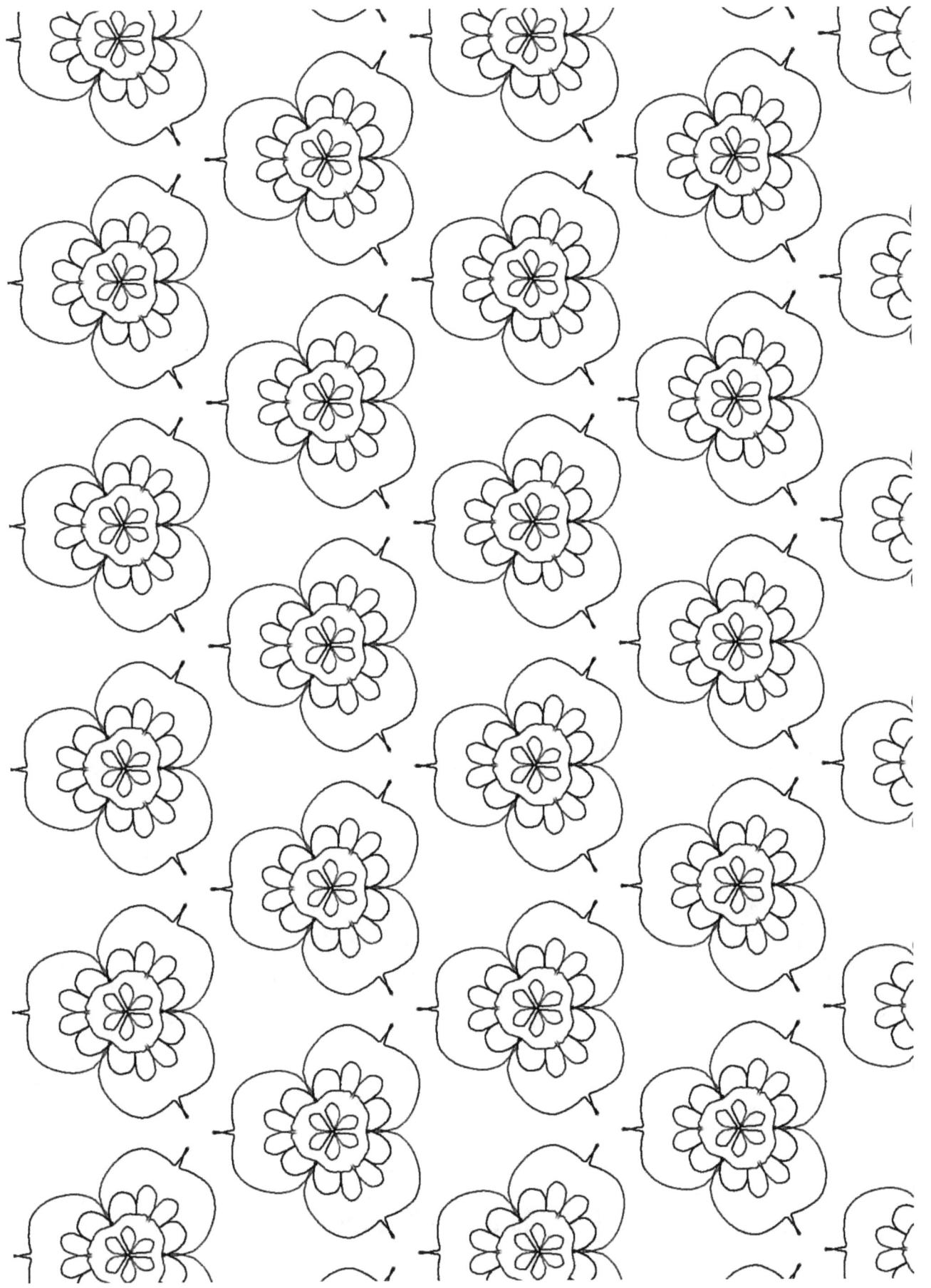

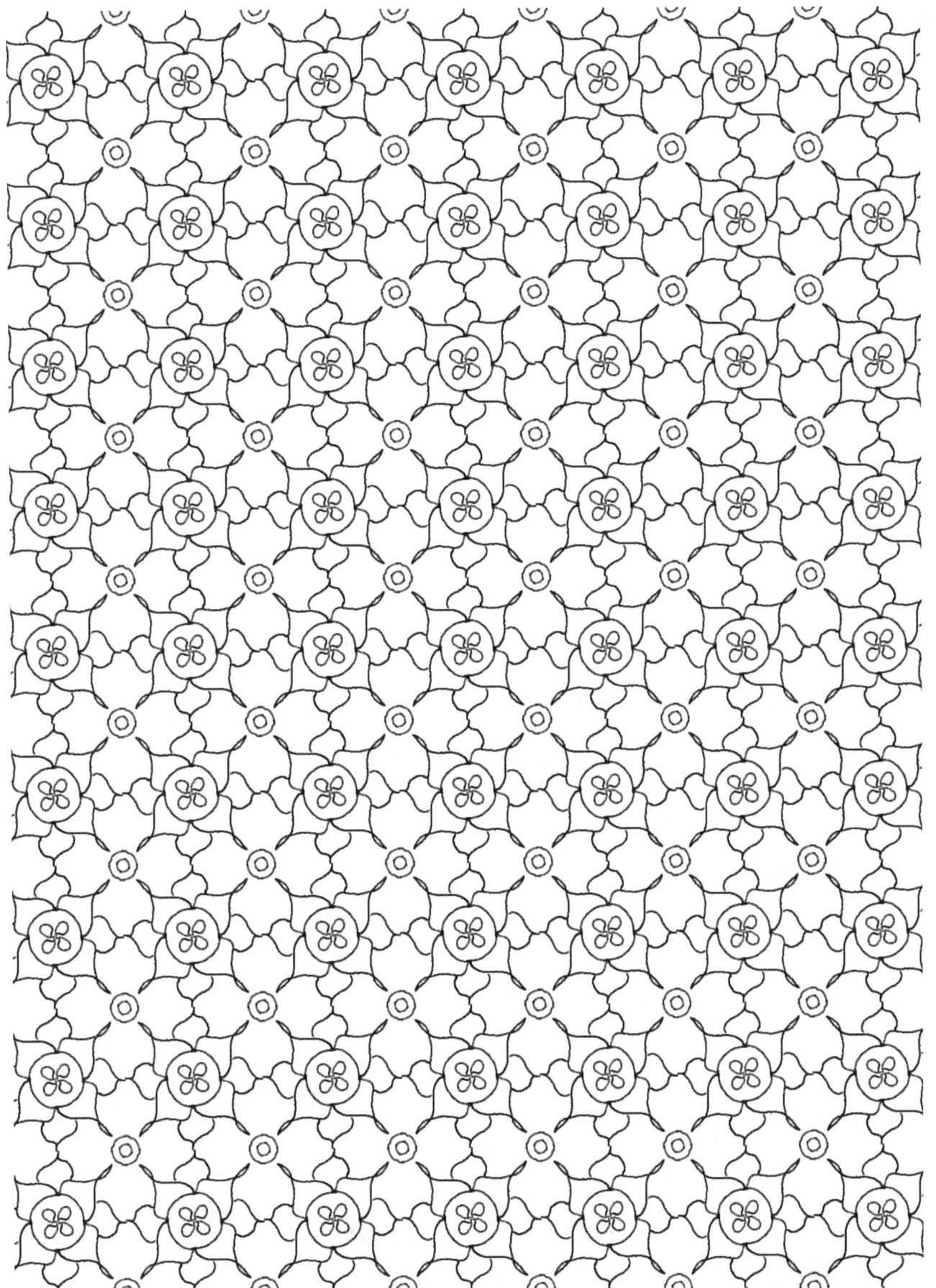

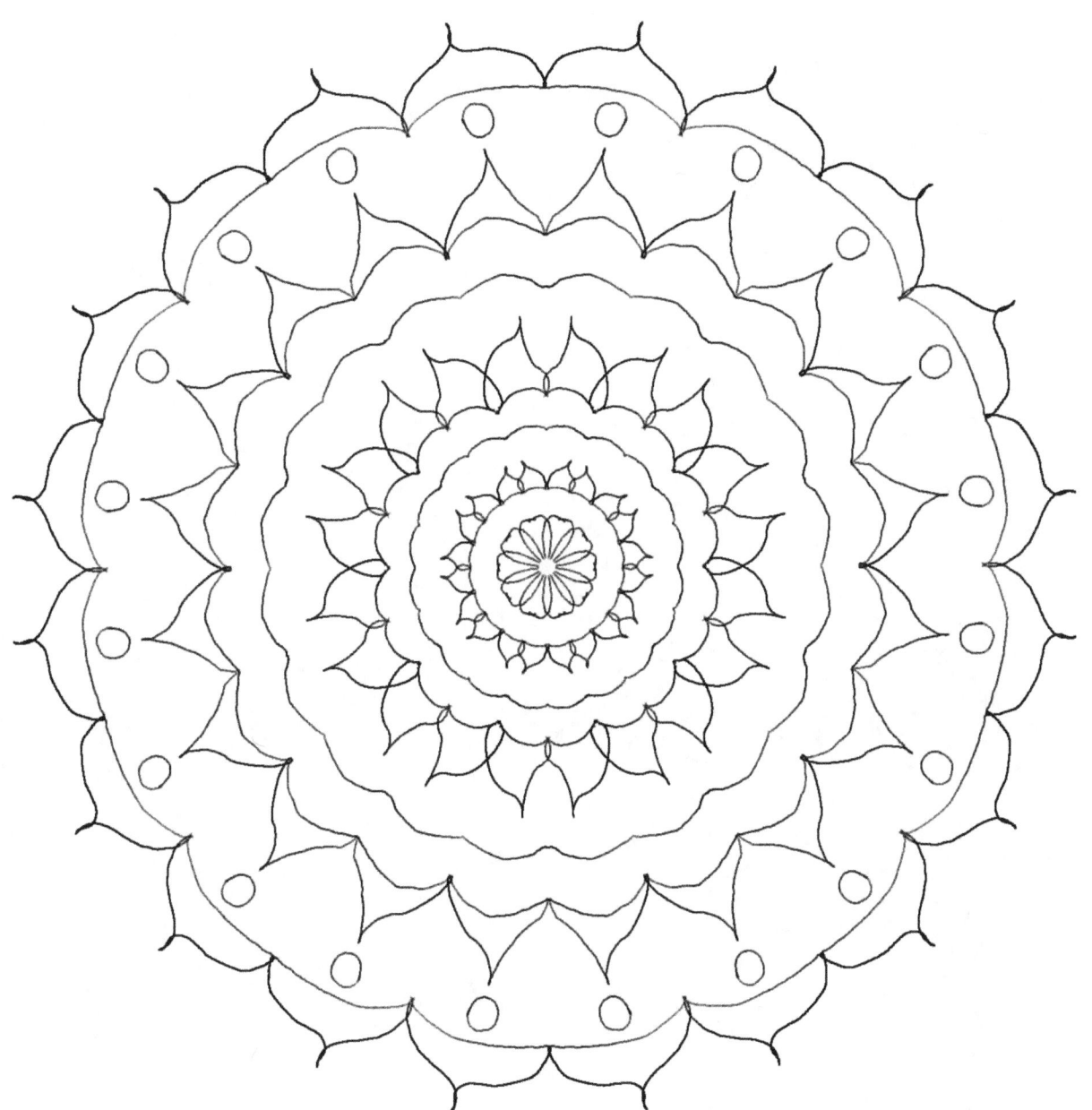

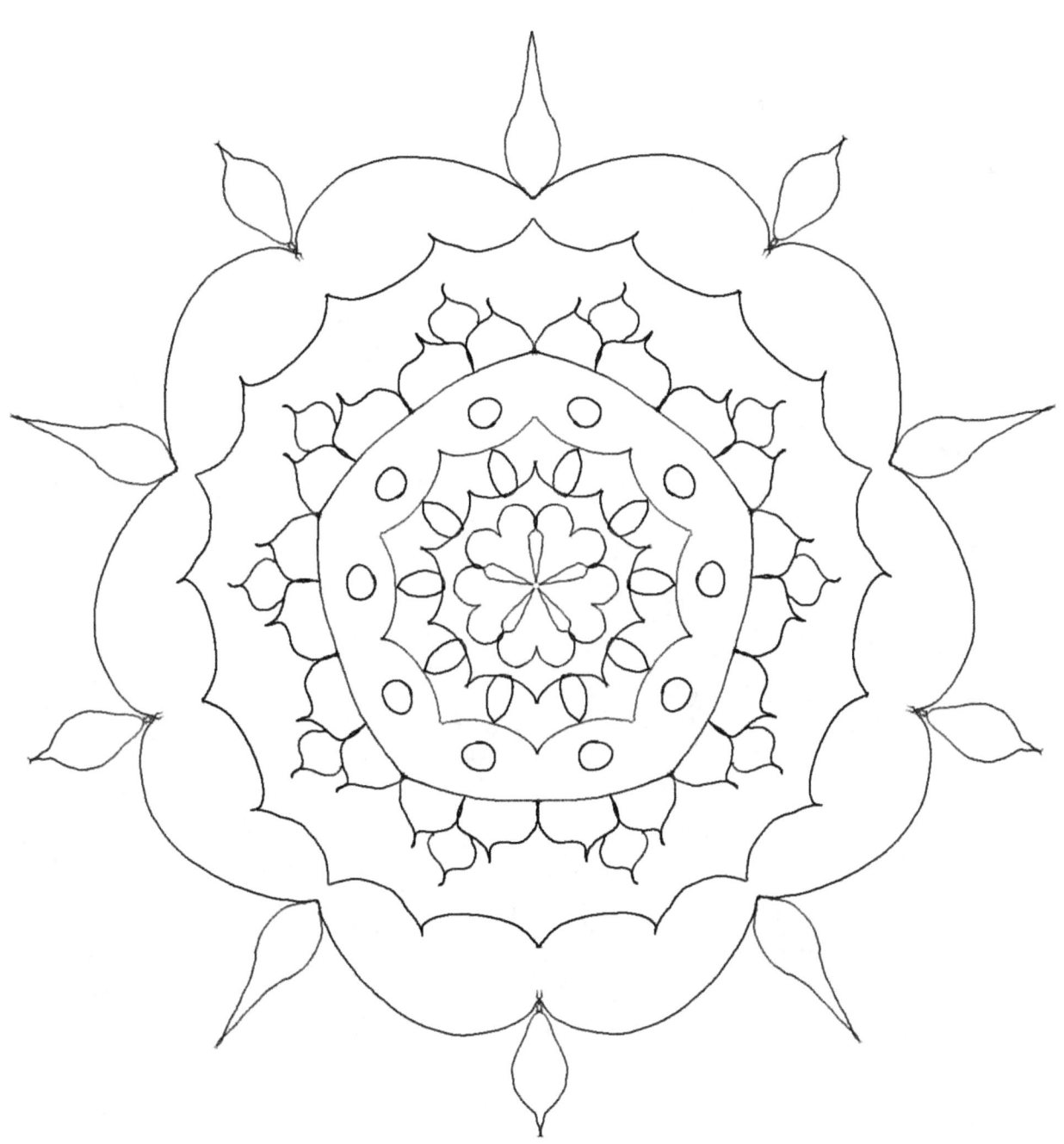

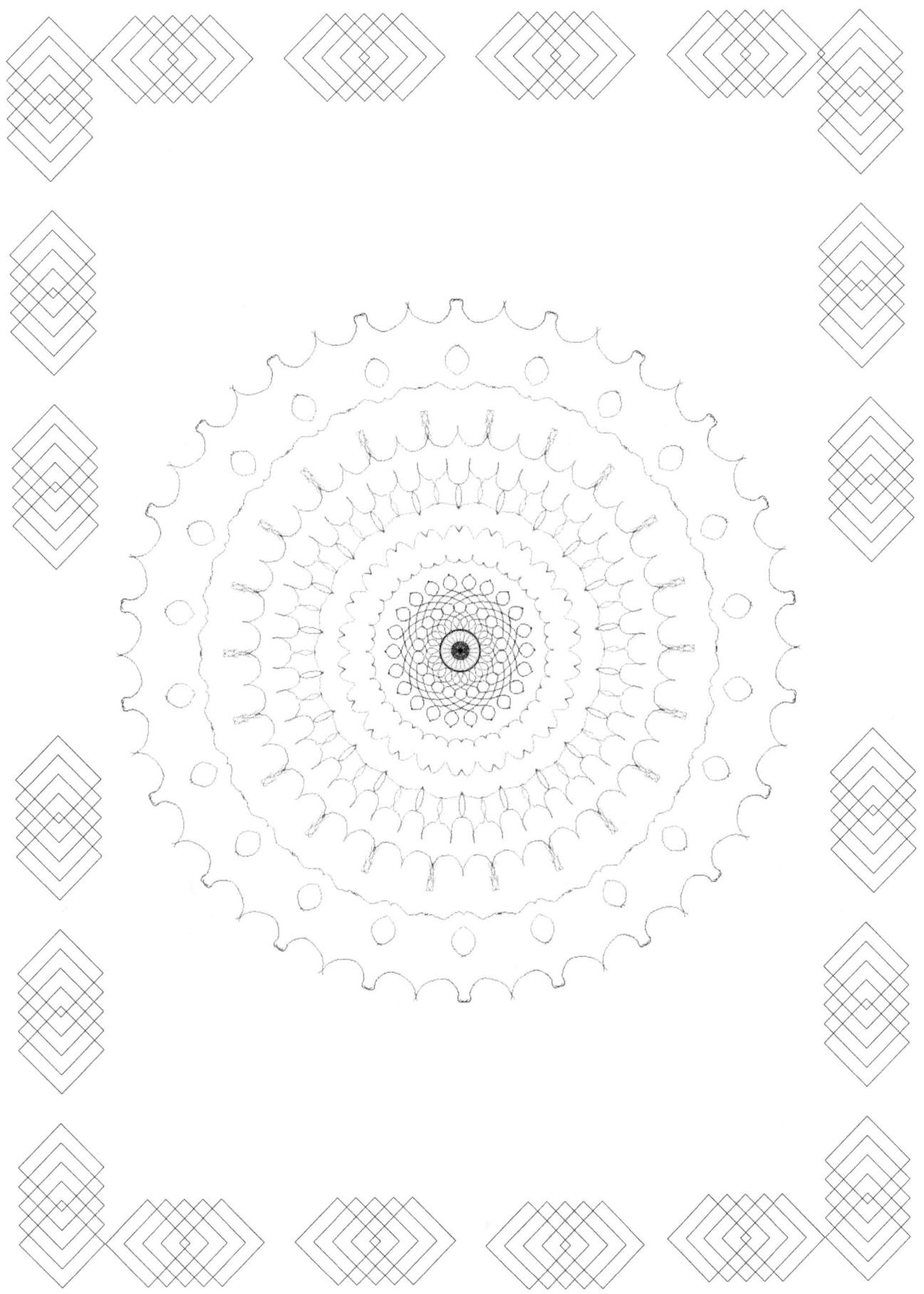

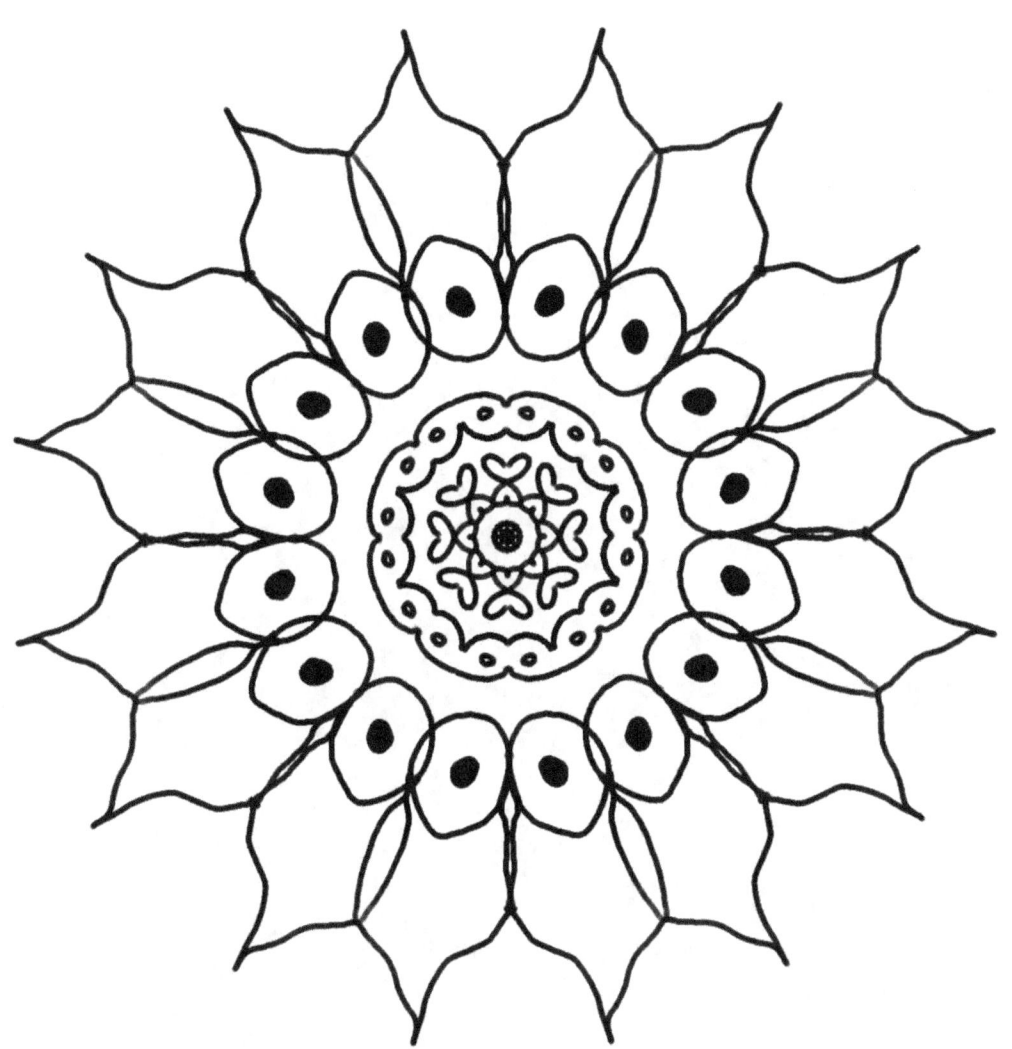

COPYRIGHT MATERIAL

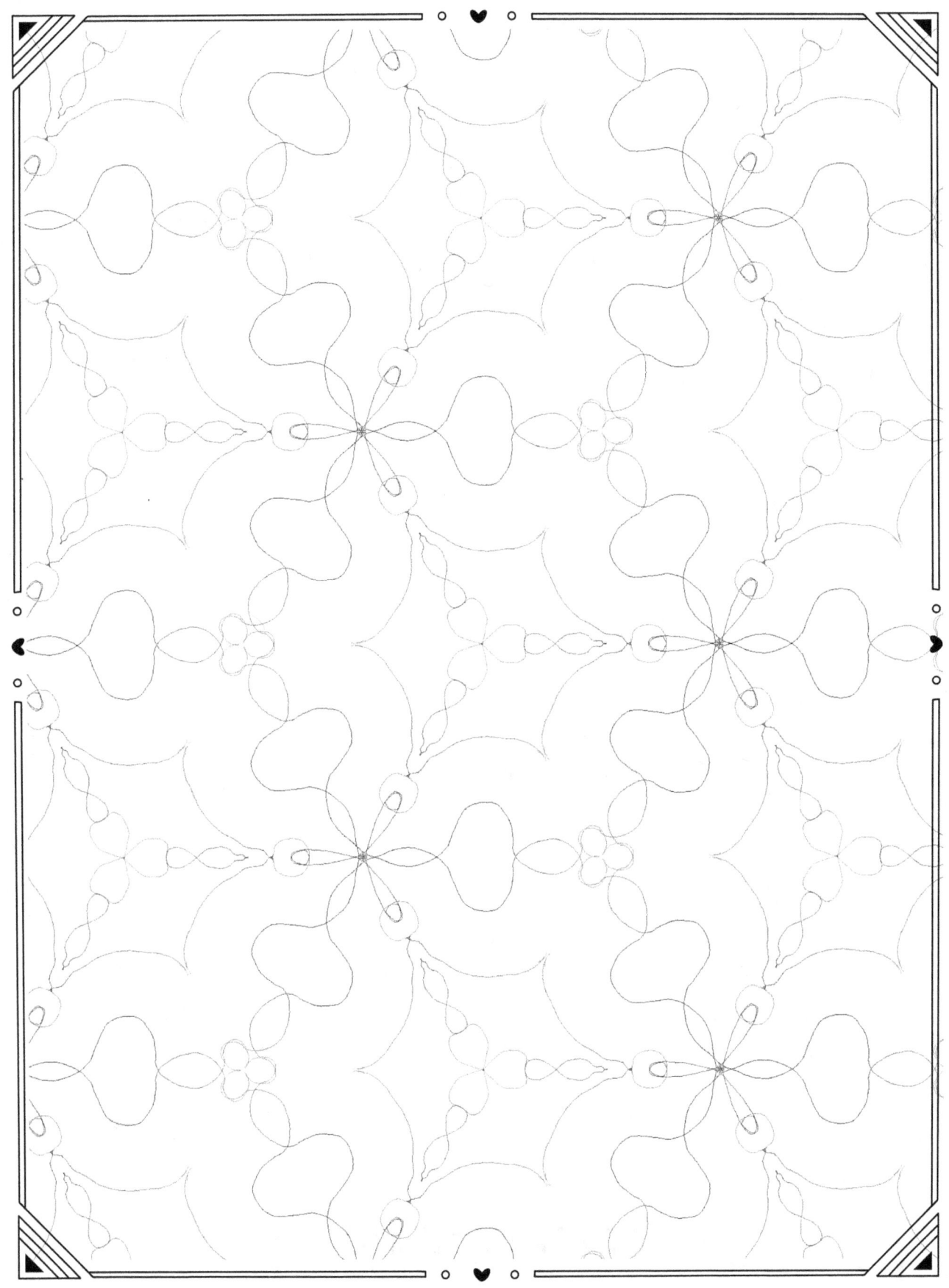

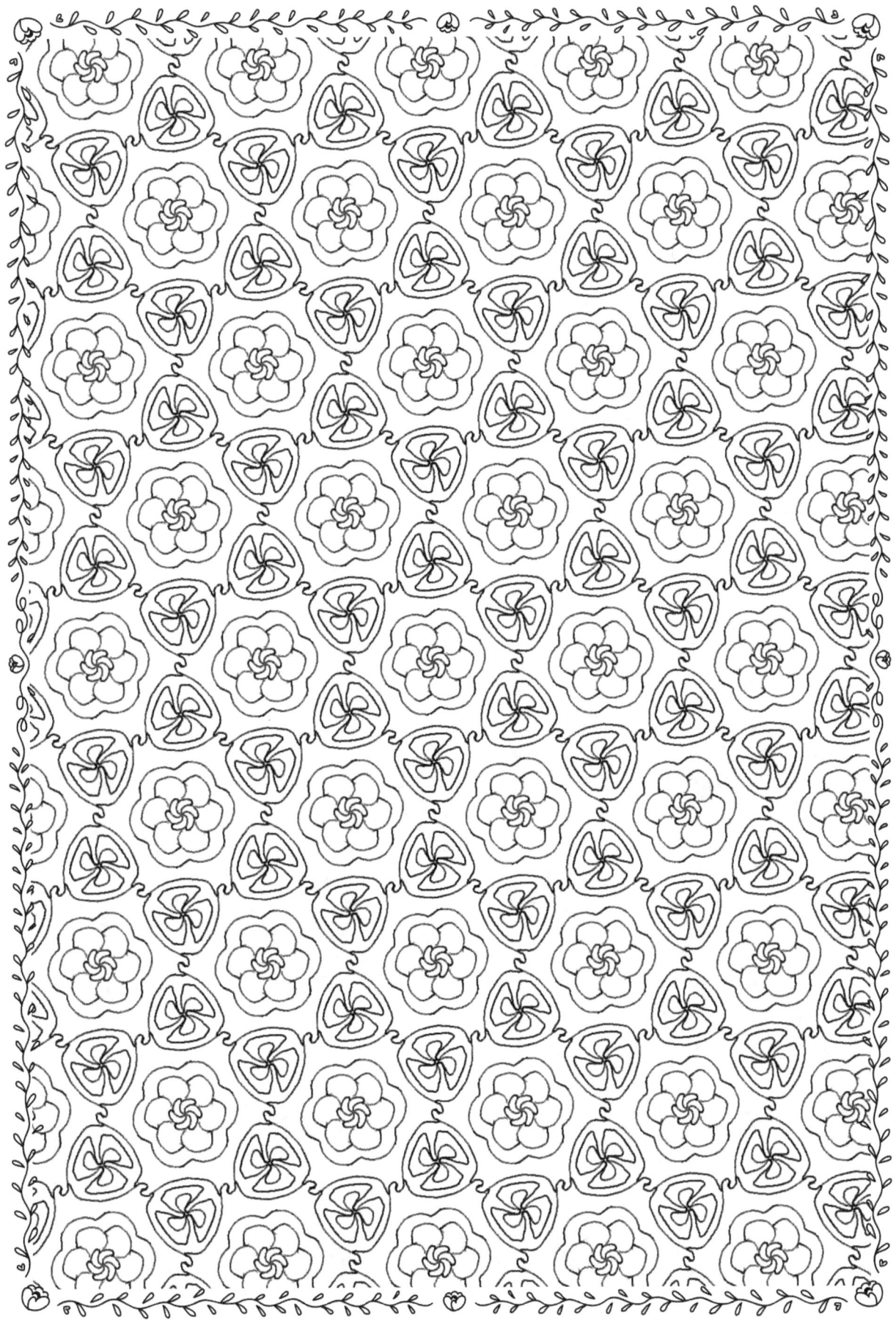

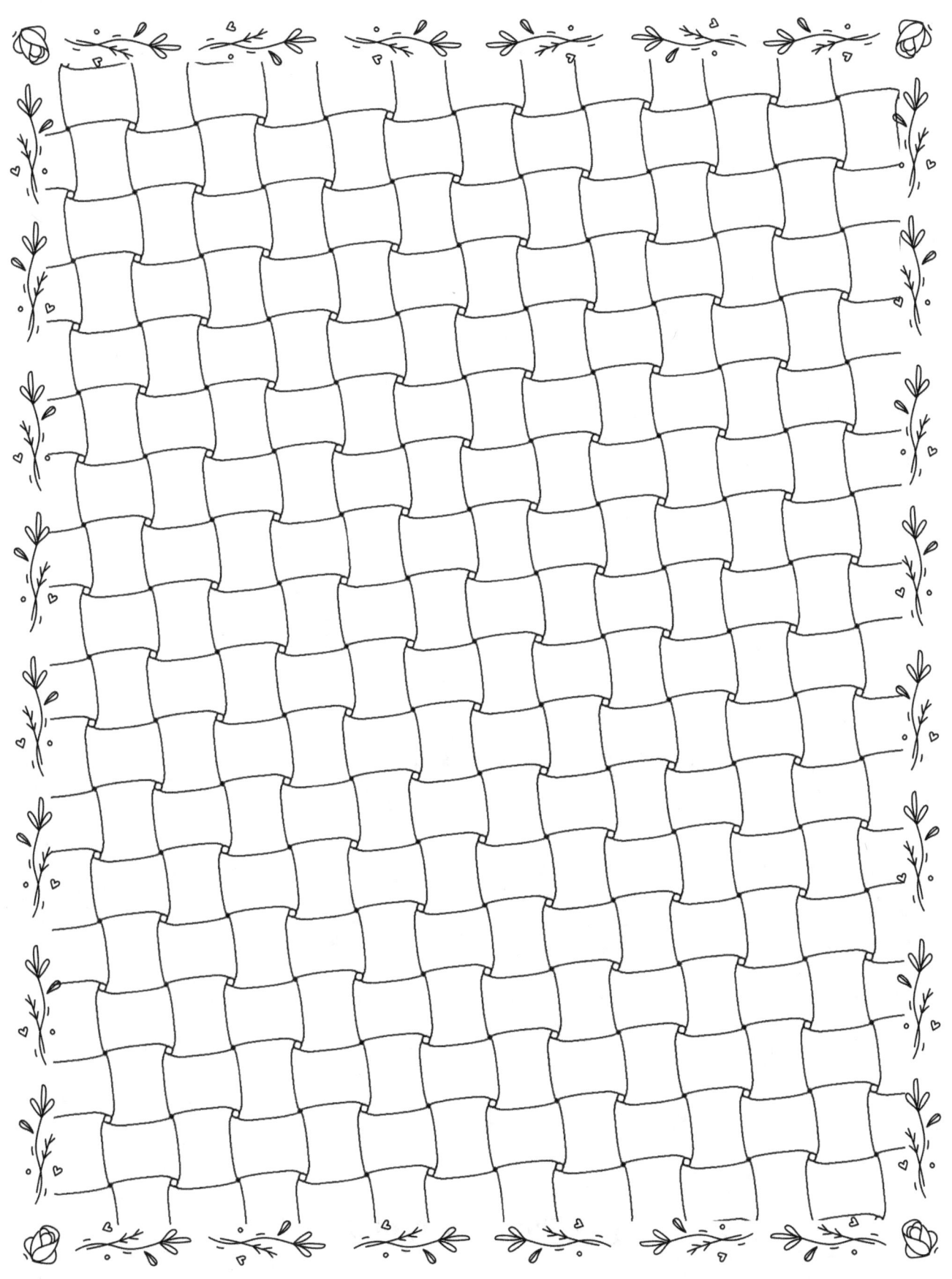

COPYRIGHT MATERIAL

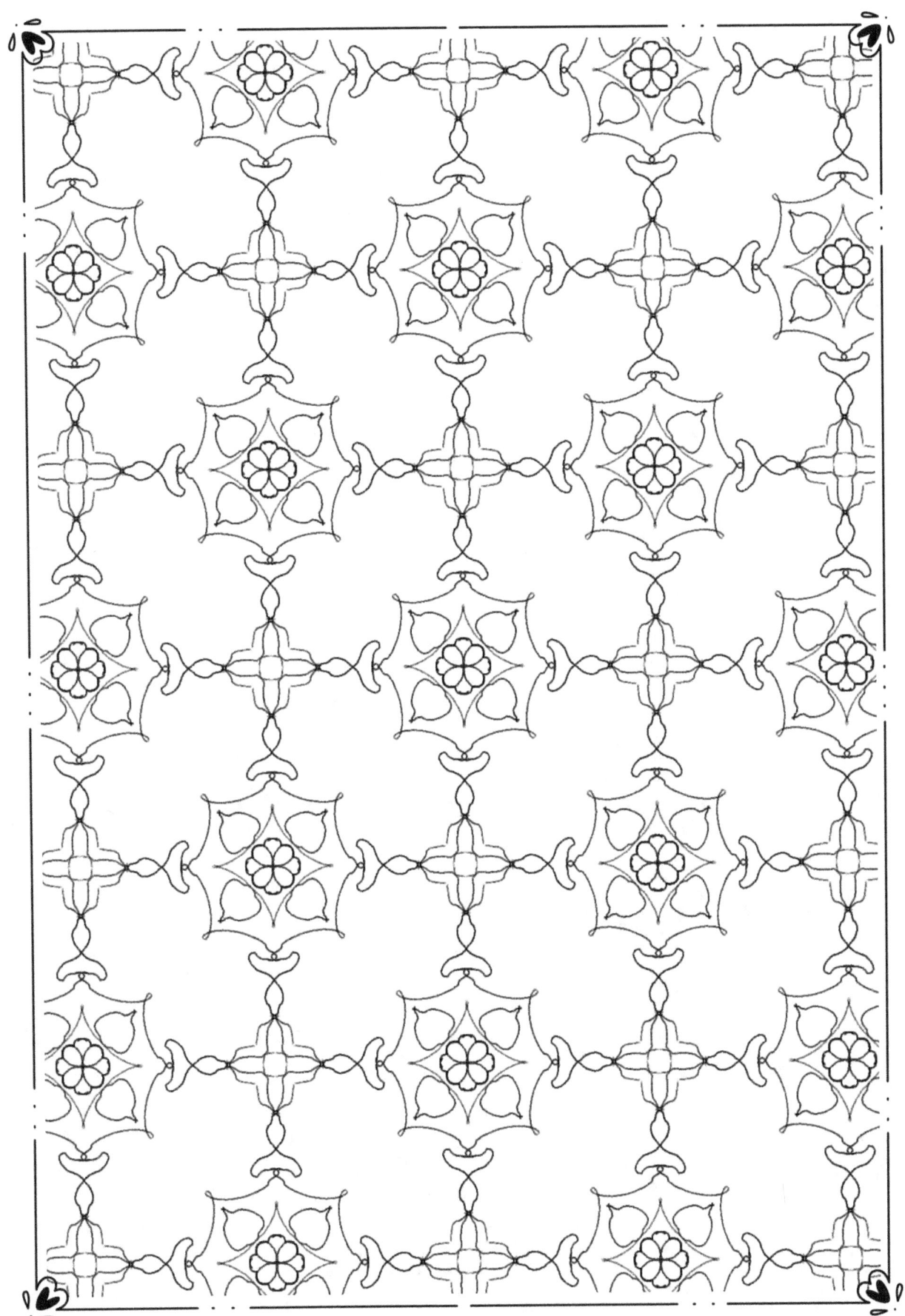

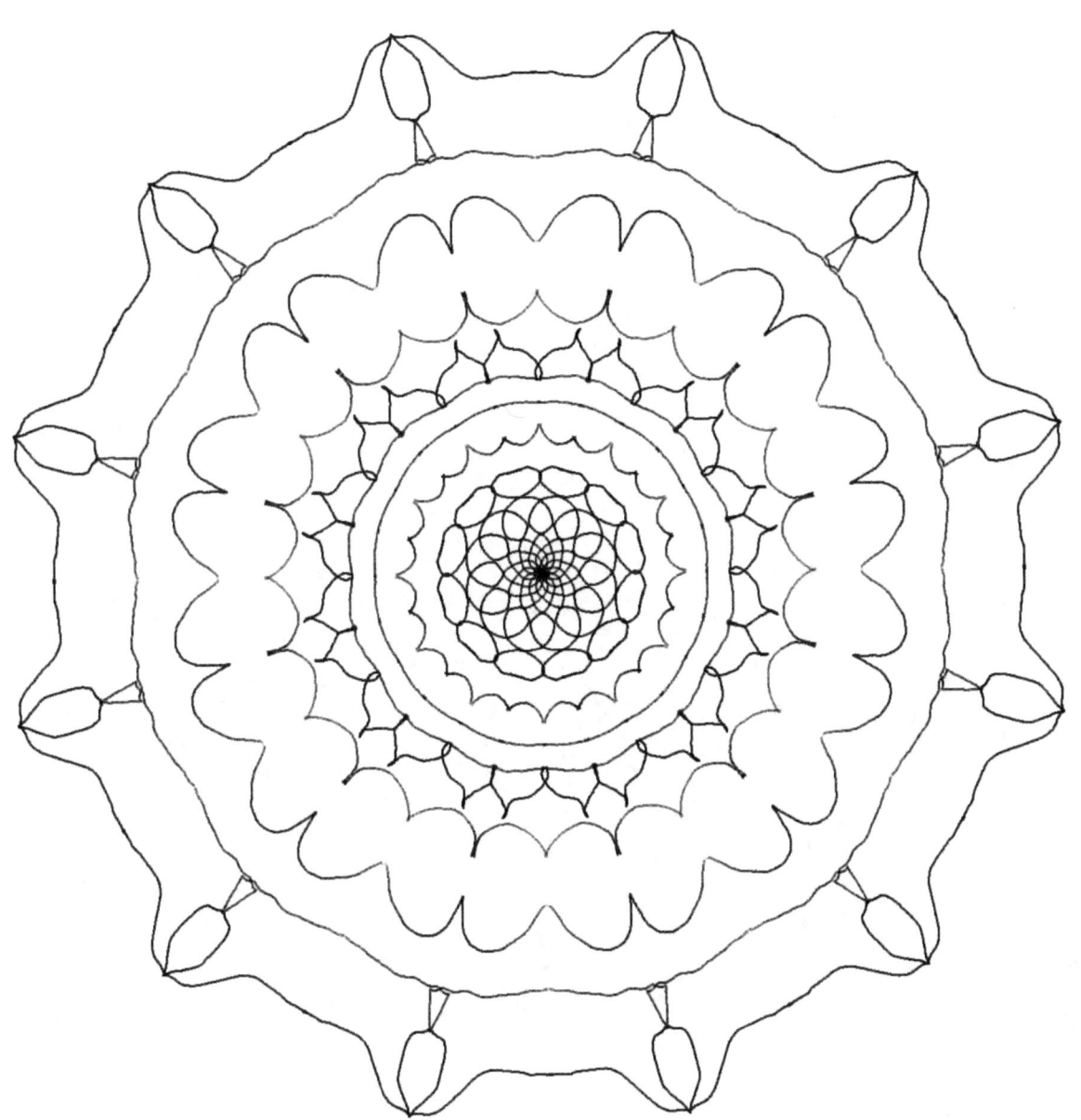

COPYRIGHT MATERIAL

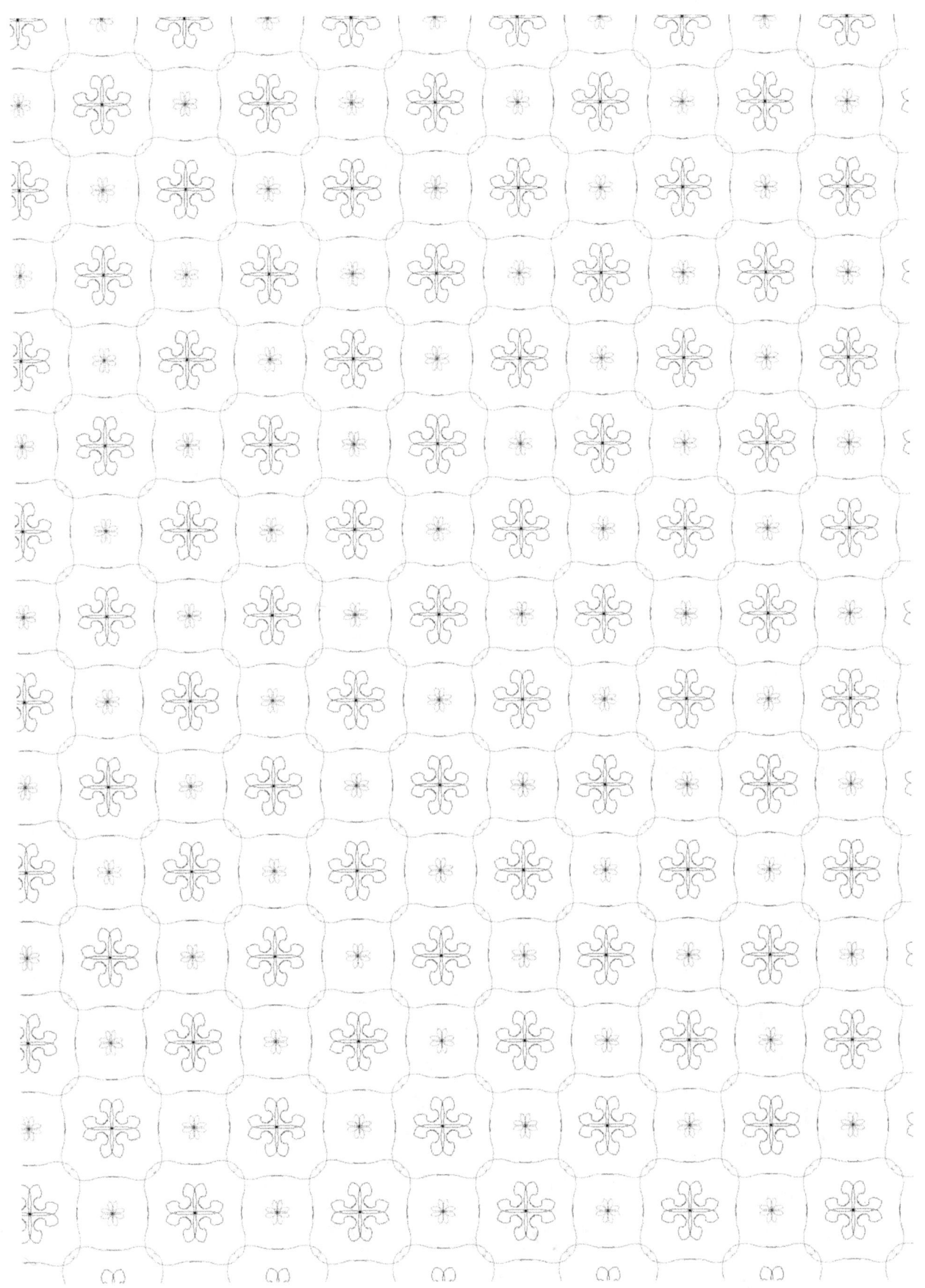

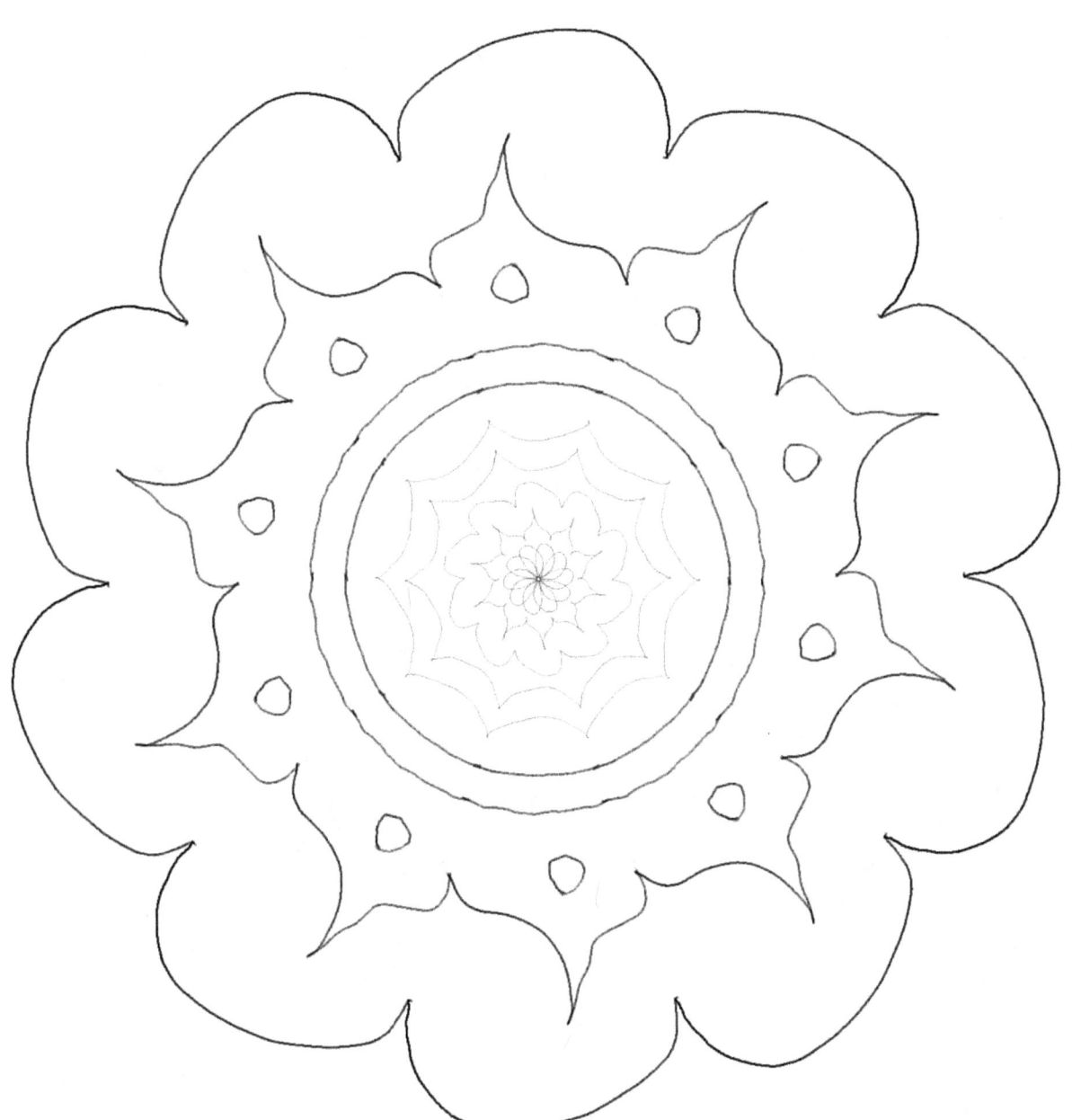

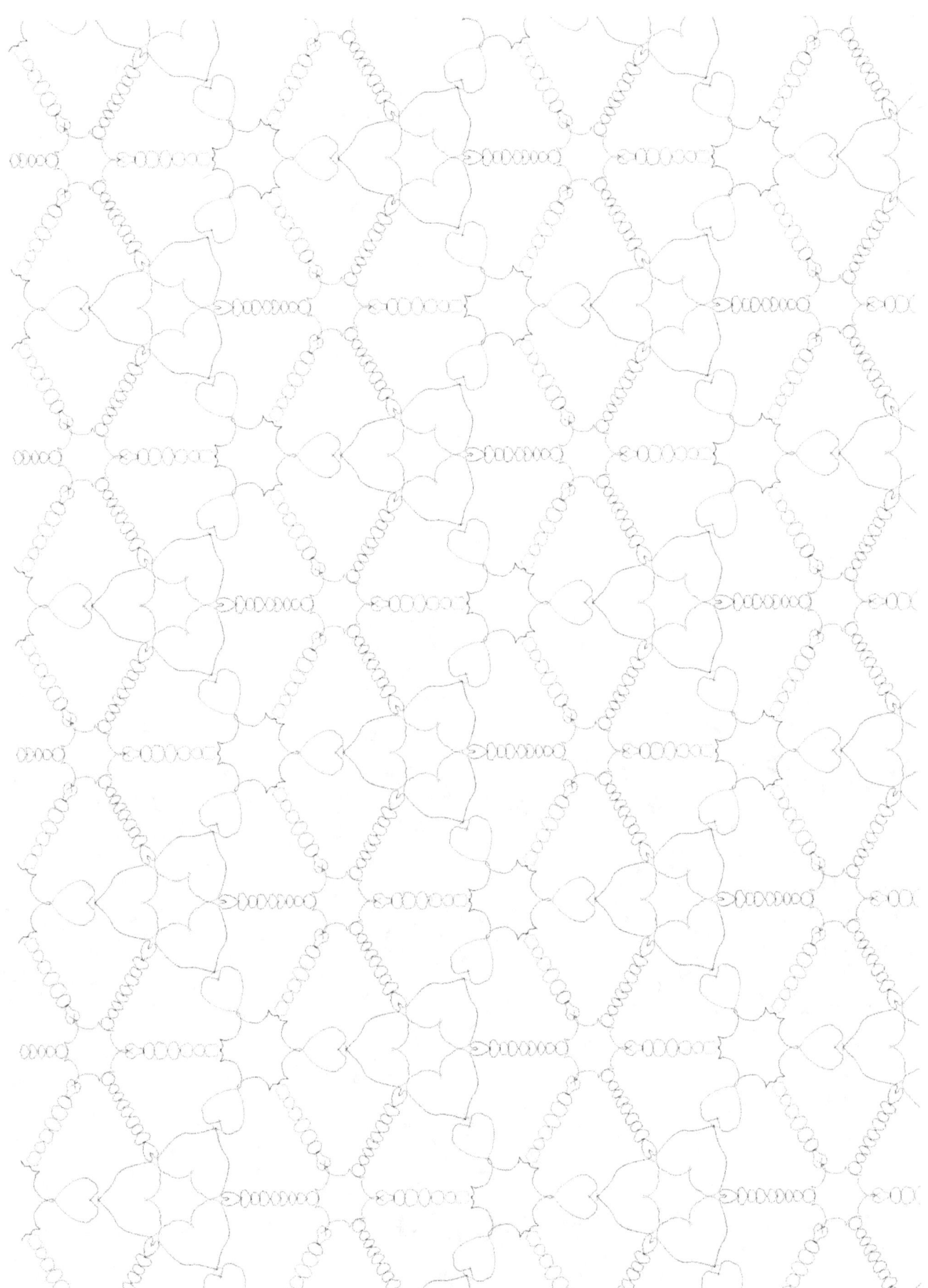

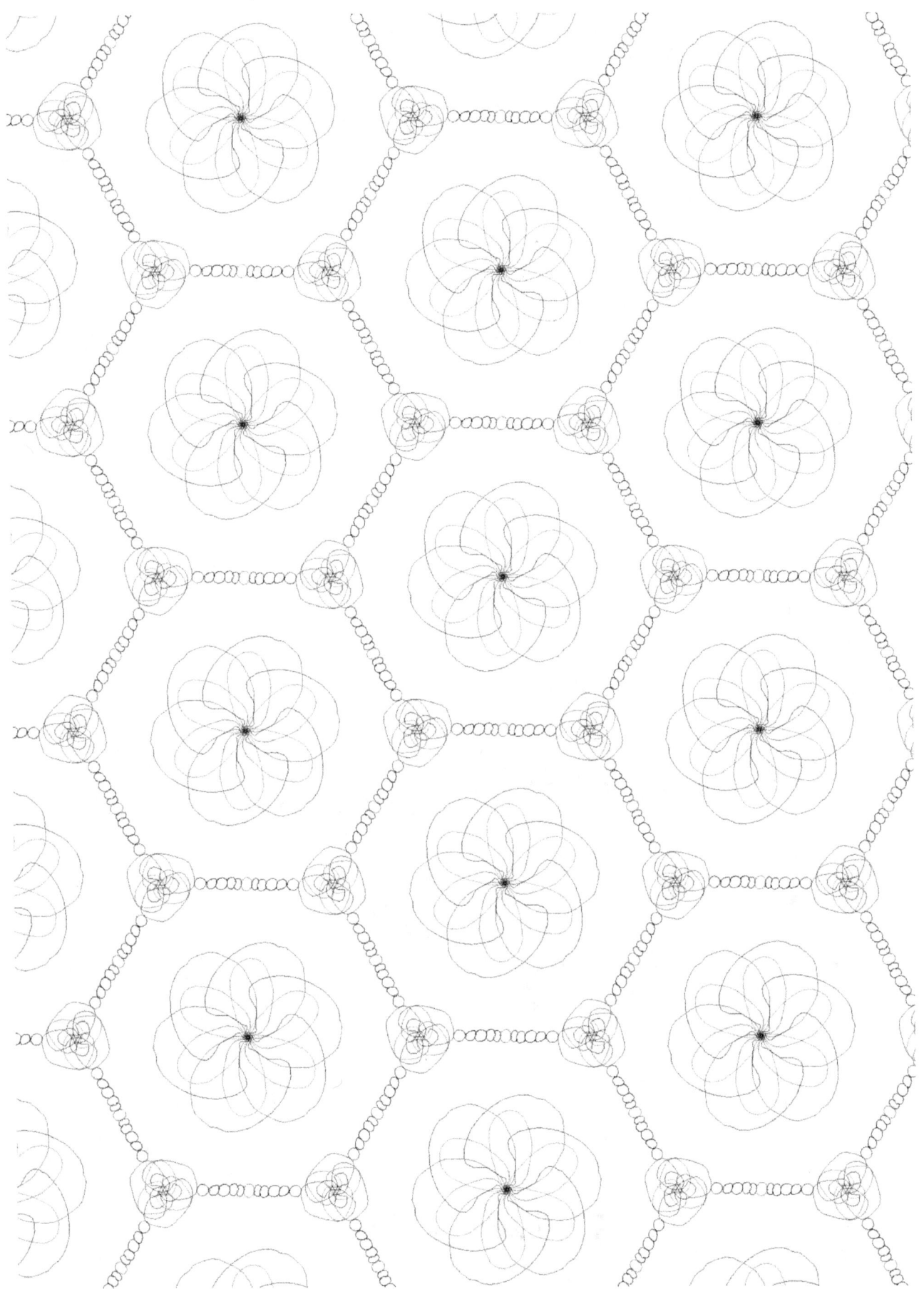

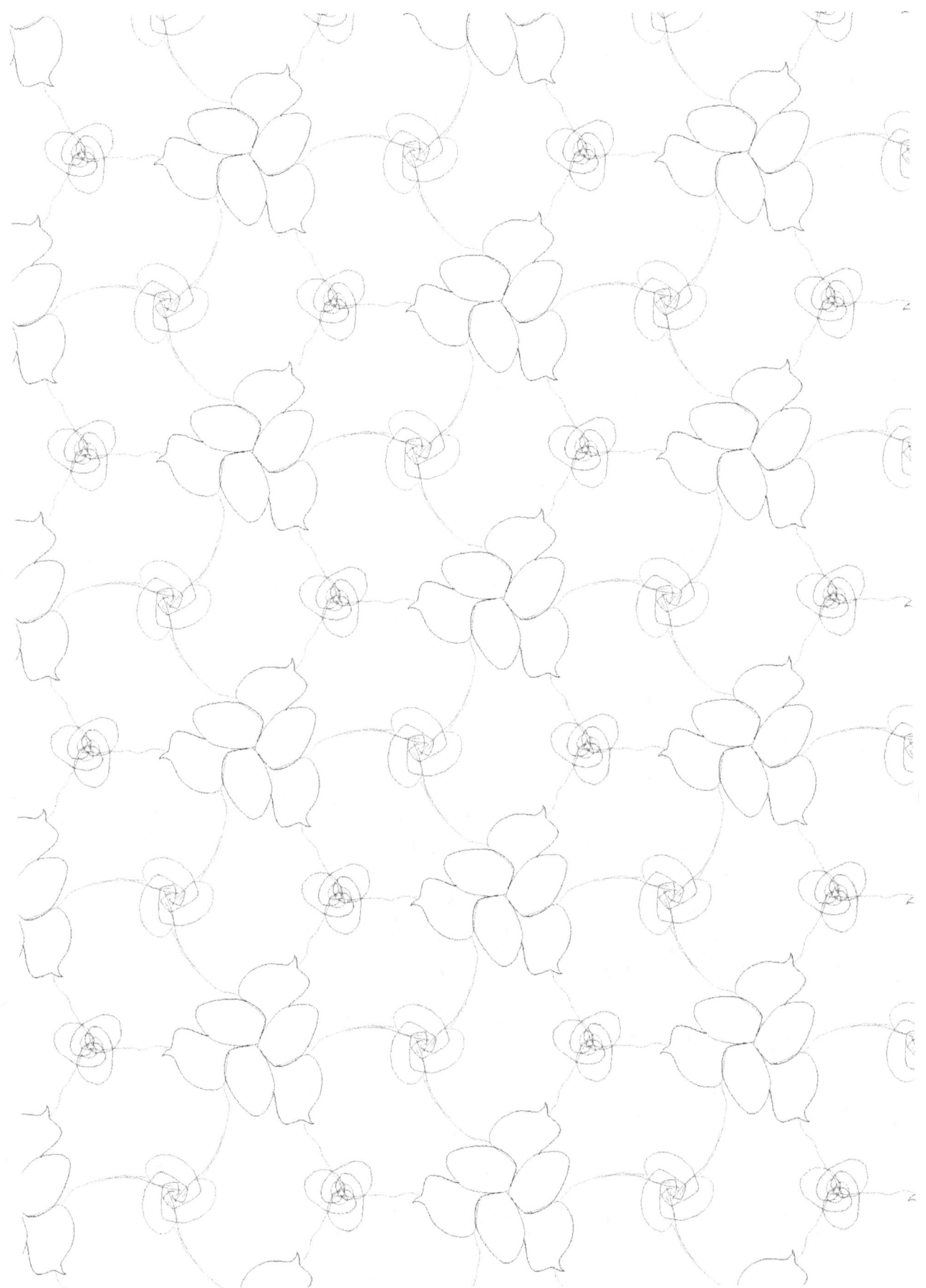

COPYRIGHT MATERIAL

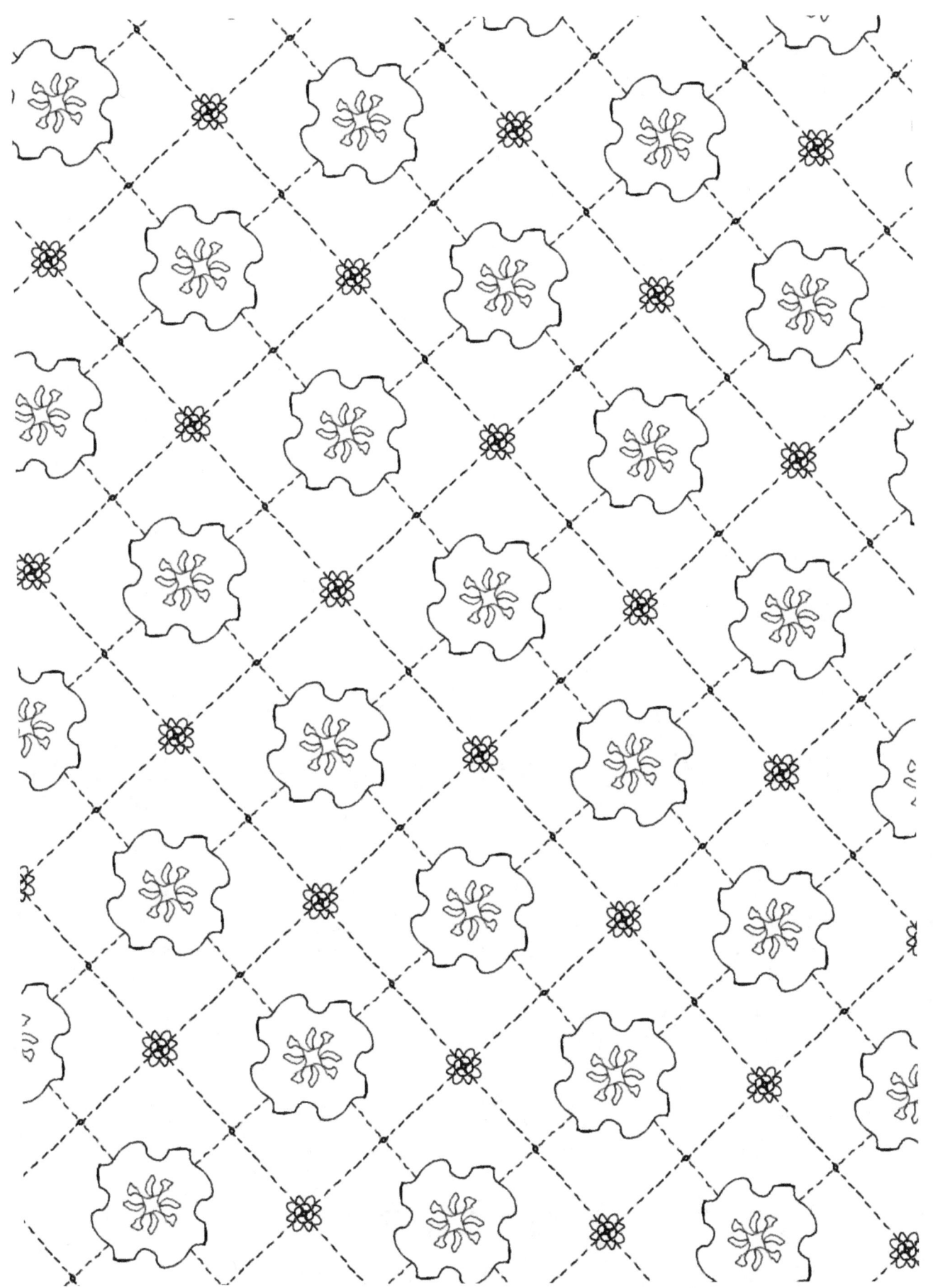

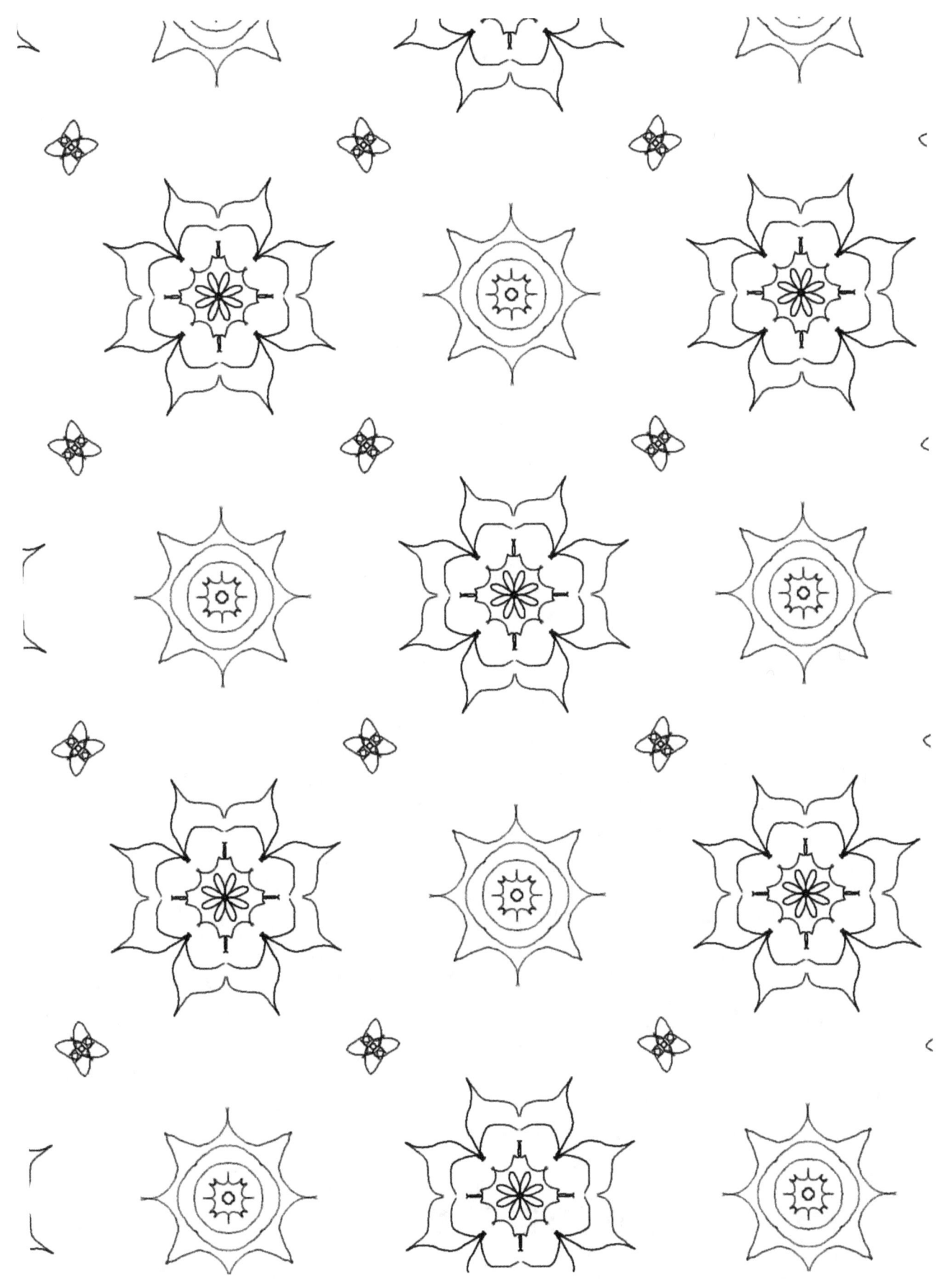

COPYRIGHT MATERIAL

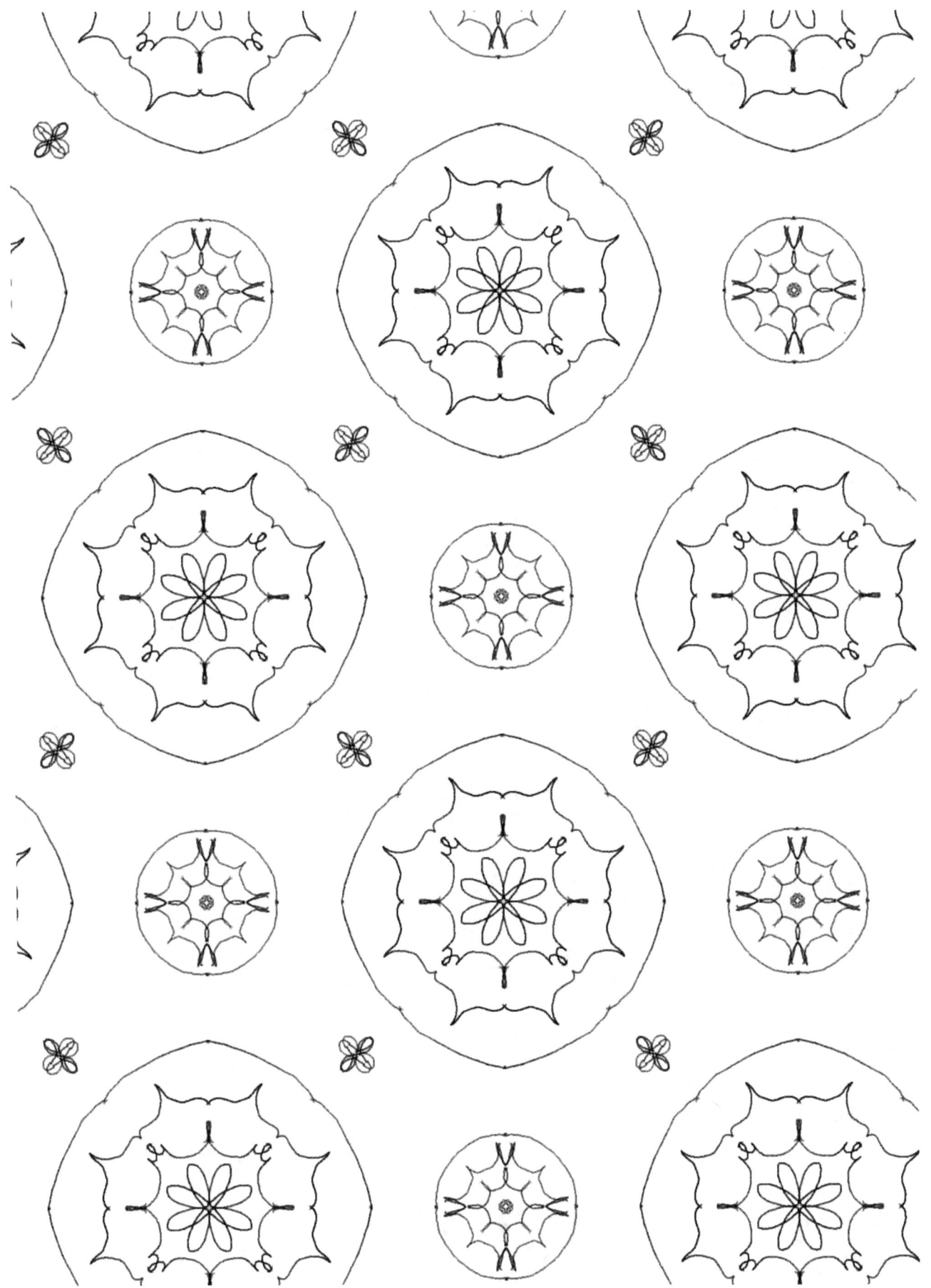

www.ingramcontent.com/pod-product-compliance
Lightning Source LLC
Chambersburg PA
CBHW081103240526
45465CB00026B/3313